JOY
COMES IN THE
MORNING
Finding Comfort In Time of Loss

BOB GASS
with
Ruth Gass Halliday

JOY COMES IN THE MORNING
Finding comfort in time of loss
ISBN 1-931727-93-7
Copyright © 2004 by Celebration Enterprises
P.O. Box 1045
Roswell, GA 30077-1045

SYNERGY PUBLISHERS
Gainesville, Florida 32635

SCRIPTURES

"Weeping may endure for a night,
but joy comes in the morning."

– *Psalm 30:5 AMP*

TABLE OF CONTENTS

"Grief is the price we pay for love."
— C.M. Parkes

1
COMING TO GRIPS WITH LOSS

*"If your heart is broken, you'll
find God right there."*
                    —Psalm 34:18 TM

On January 16th, 2003, Evelyn Husband lost her life's partner, Commander Rick Husband, when the space shuttle Columbia disintegrated over the Texas skyline killing everyone aboard. Standing in stunned disbelief at the landing site, she remembers her seven-year-old, Matthew, asking, "Does this mean I won't be going to Indian Guides with Dad anymore?" And twelve-year-old Laura wanting to know, "Who'll walk me down the aisle some day, Mom? Or help me with my math homework?"

Following the incident Evelyn talked openly about how the faith she'd found as a teenager was still sustaining her. When interviewed she told the world she was trusting God for strength and quoted Proverbs 3:5-6, "Trust in the Lord with all thine heart; and lean not unto thine own understanding. In all thy ways acknowledge him, and he shall direct thy paths."

Addressing a women's conference she said, "Most of you aren't going to lose the person you love most on national television. But every one here will face big tragedies and little everyday crises. And your only consistency is Jesus Christ." Her message was this: *even in the midst of intense suffering, God is faithful.*

For Evelyn, the moments of unexpected grief were the hardest. She said, "One day I walked into a grocery store and saw a magazine with a picture of Rick on the front. Above it was a headline that read, 'The Last Seven Horrifying Minutes for the Space Shuttle Crew.' By the time I checked out I was a hysterical, sobbing mess. Going to the store is still one of the hardest things for me."

But the same pain that makes those everyday tasks so emotionally draining, has become the bridge over which she walks to help others struggling with grief. Evelyn didn't make it this far by turning out the lights and crawling under the bedcovers. Instead, by mustering the courage to take one tiny step of faith at a time, she discovered that what she'd always known about God in her *head*, is true in *reality*. She says, "In light of what happened you'd think I'd be disillusioned with God, but strangely it hasn't been that way at all. I've learned that Jesus was a Man of sorrows who's well acquainted with my grief. He knows how deeply I'm hurting and He's been with me every moment. This situation has given me a chance to honor Him before others, and that's what I'm trying to do."

A pastor who returned to his pulpit ten days after his son's suicide, spoke on Romans 8:28, "We know that God causes all things to work together for good to those who love [Him]" (NASB). Visibly struggling, he said, "I've tried to make my son's suicide fit into this passage and I can't. I just don't see how anything good can come out of it. Yet I realize that according to God's Word, everything I know at this moment is partial and incomplete (See 1Co 13:12 NLT).

"It's like the miracle of the shipyard," he continued, "almost every part of our great ocean-going vessels is made of steel. If you take any single part, be it a steel plate from the hull or the huge rudder, and throw it into the ocean, it'll sink. Steel doesn't float. But when the shipbuilder is finished and the last plate has been riveted in place, that massive ship is virtually unsinkable.

"Taken by itself my son's suicide is senseless. However, I know that when God has worked out His perfect design, even *this* seemingly senseless tragedy will turn out for our good."

Many of us are familiar with Don Moen's praise song, *"God Will Make a Way."* But most of us don't know the story behind it. Several years ago Don was wakened during the night when his mother-in-law called to tell him about a car accident involving his wife's sister Susan. She, her husband Craig and their four little boys were on a trip when tragedy struck. Jeremy, age-eight, was killed instantly. The others were seriously injured. Don felt helpless to bring hope and comfort to Susan and Craig. What could he possibly say? Then God gave him these words:

> God will make a way when there seems to be no way.
>
> He works in ways we cannot see. He will make a way for me.
>
> He will be my guide; hold me closely to His side.
>
> With love and strength for each new day, He will make a way.

Eric Liddell, whose life story was told in the movie *Chariots of Fire*, writes, "Circumstances may appear to wreck our lives and God's plans, but God isn't helpless among the ruins. Our broken lives aren't lost or useless; God is still working. He comes in, takes the calamity and uses it, working out His wonderful plan of love."

Because a funeral was a time to demonstrate grief, in Jesus' day it was considered a sign of respect to weep loudly. And because the mourners were powerless to change what had happened, it was also the time they felt most helpless and vulnerable.

When Jesus arrived at Bethany, His friend Lazarus had died and Mary his sister was upset because Jesus hadn't come sooner. She said, "Lord, if You had been here, my brother would not have died" (Jn 11:32 NASB). So how did He react? The Bible says that sitting down among the mourners, "Jesus wept" (Jn 11:35).

Did He weep because He was powerless in the situation? No. He knew Lazarus would soon be alive again. He also knew that at His Second Coming Lazarus and every other believer will be resurrected to spend eternity with Him in heaven. The Bible says, "When Jesus...saw [Mary]...and the Jews who came with her...weeping, He was deeply moved" (Jn 11:33 NASB).

Jesus wept because He's touched by the heartache of those He loves!

Author Edgar Jackson writes, "Grief is a young widow trying to raise her three children alone. It's a man so filled with shocked uncertainty and confusion that he strikes out at the nearest person. It's a mother walking daily to a cemetery to stand alone for a few minutes before going about the tasks of the day; she knows part of her is in that cemetery just as part of her is in her daily work. Grief is a knife-like pain that comes a hundred times a day when you start to speak to someone who's no longer there;

it's the emptiness of eating alone after eating with another for many years. It's learning to go to bed without saying goodnight; it's wishing things were different when you know they're not and never will be again. Grief is a whole cluster of adjustments and uncertainties that strike life in its forward progress, making it feel almost impossible to redirect your energies."

C.M Parks said, *"Grief is the price we pay for love." The only ones who escape it are those who have never loved.*

Nancy Guthrie writes, "Not long after my six-month-old daughter, Hope, died, I was at a cosmetics counter buying mascara. 'Will this run down my face when I cry?' I asked. The girl behind the counter assured me it wouldn't, and asked with a smile, 'Why, are you gonna be crying?' 'Yes,' I answered. 'I am.'

"We had Hope for one hundred and ninety-nine days. We loved her. We enjoyed her richly and shared her with everyone we could. We held her during her seizures. Then we let her go. The day after we buried her my husband said, 'I think we expected our faith to make this hurt less but it doesn't. It gave us strength and encouragement while she was alive and we're comforted by the knowledge that she's in heaven. It keeps us from being swallowed up by despair, but I don't think it makes our loss hurt any less.'

"People often ask, 'How are you?' And for the first year my answer was, 'I'm deeply and profoundly sad.' I've been blessed with many people willing to share my sorrow, to just be sad with me. Others, however, seem to want to rush me through my sadness. They want to fix me. Ours isn't a culture that's comfortable with sadness. Sadness is awkward...unsettling. It ebbs and flows and takes its own shape. It beckons to be shared. It comes out in tears, and we don't quite know what to do with those tears. Many people are afraid to bring up my loss. They don't want to upset me. But tears are the only way I have to release the sorrow I feel. So I tell them, 'don't worry about crying in front of me, and don't be afraid you'll make me cry. *Your* tears tell me you care. *My* tears tell you that you've touched me...and I'll never forget your willingness to share my grief.'"

How do we mourn? Author, Melody Beattie says, "We do it awkwardly, imperfectly, with resistance, anger and attempts to negotiate. We flounder through kicking and screaming until we reach the place of *acceptance*."

Tears don't represent a lack of faith; they just mean you're human. The One who gave you the ability to love, understands loss; that's why He gave you tears.

When Jesus wept at Lazarus' funeral, He made it okay for us to cry too!

Even though the Bible says, "The Lord is close to the brokenhearted" (Ps 34:18), sometimes it's hard to see how He can relate to our circumstances. If that's how you feel today, listen: "He had to enter into every detail of human life. Then, when he came before God as high priest...he would have already experienced...all the pain, all the testing – and...be able to help" (Heb 2:17-18 TM). Jesus walked the path you're on so that you could go to Him at anytime, knowing He understands and "is able to help."

Recently I read about a man who underwent open-heart surgery. He said, "The day before my surgery a lovely nurse came into my room to visit me. She took me by the hand and said, 'During the surgery tomorrow you'll be disconnected from your heart and kept alive by machines. When the operation is over you'll awaken in the recovery room but you won't be able to move for about six hours. You won't be able to speak or even open your eyes, but you'll be perfectly conscious. You'll hear and know everything that's going on around you. That can be frightening. So during those hours I'll stay by your side and hold your hand as I am right now. I'll be with you until you're fully recovered. If you become anxious or afraid, just feel the touch of my hand on yours and know that you're not alone, for I won't leave you.' And it happened exactly as she said. I awoke, and even though I could do nothing, just the touch of her hand on mine made all the difference!"

What a picture! Jesus' favorite word for the Holy Spirit was Paraclete – "one who stands beside to help." Engrave those words on your mind until they're such a part of you that regardless of what you're going through, you'll know with certainty that God's love is surrounding you, sustaining you, and strengthening you.

You're His child and that's His promise to you!

But while God "heals the brokenhearted," (Ps 147:3 NLT), He also recognizes that mourning is an important part of closure. That's why He never promised to preserve us *from* loss, but to bring us *through* it. When you've lost someone you love there's no quick fix. The only way out, is through!

One woman said, "I'd no idea grieving involved so many 'firsts'...my first night alone...the first time I attended church alone...my first anniversary alone. And just when I thought things couldn't get worse, I find myself facing the holidays alone...I'd give anything to boycott them."

If that's how you feel, here are a few suggestions:

Network with others. As part of a group you discover that you're not alone; that mourning isn't a sickness or self-indulgence; that sharing with those who've walked in your shoes can bring healing.

Don't try to deny your loss. The Bible says, "The memory of the just is blessed" (Pr 10:7). When you're around others don't be afraid to talk about your loss. When you do, you send a signal that it's okay for them to share their memories too.

Expand your "family." Solomon writes, "Better a nearby friend than a distant family" (Pr 27:10 TM). Going it alone usually means going nowhere. Even though it feels uncomfortable reach out to friends and loved ones; ask them to pray with and for you. And remember, others don't know what you need unless you tell them.

Don't try to do it all yourself. The Bible says, "There's a time to cry" (Ecc 3:4 NLT). Because grief is so draining you may need more rest than usual. So let others help you with the everyday stuff like cooking, cleaning and paying bills till you feel stronger. And don't forget, those who spend time with the Lord...renew their strength (See Is 40:29,31), so reach for Him when you're feeling down.

Care for yourself physically. When you've experienced great loss you often lack the energy to take care of yourself. You're too busy surviving. So to understand your body's needs, use the acronym

D.E.E.R. (D-rink, E-at, E-xercise, R-est) to help you stay focused.

Protect your boundaries. You know better than anybody else how you're feeling. So whenever you're not up to visiting or going out to dinner with friends, give yourself permission to say, "No thanks, I'll take a rain check." This is one area where you can exercise some control over your life.

Whenever possible, plan ahead. There's no "right" or "wrong" way to handle special events like birthdays, memorials and holidays. Many people decide to do something different instead of trying to maintain old traditions. Just do whatever's right for you, without feeling guilty.

Don't expect too much too soon. The Bible says, "Don't be anxious – God will take care of your tomorrow...Live one day at a time" (Mt 6:34 TLB). Take it a day at a time and try to maintain reasonable expectations about what you can and can't handle right now. In other words, treat yourself like you'd treat your best friend, by being kind, patient and nurturing.

*"There is nothing – no circumstances,
no trouble, no testing – that can ever touch
me until it has gone past God, and if it
has come that far it has come with a great
purpose, which I may not understand at
the moment. But as I lift up my eyes to
Him and accept it as coming from the
throne of God, no sorrow will ever
destroy me, no trial disarm me, no
circumstance cause me to fret, for I
shall rest in the joy of what my Lord is."*

– Alan Redpath

2

KNOWING WHOSE HAND YOU'RE HOLDING

"Thus far has the Lord helped us."
– 1 Samuel 7:12 NIV

It was an exciting day in the camp of Israel when God's people miraculously crossed over the River Jordan and on to dry land. But God knows how quickly we forget, so he told Joshua to take twelve stones from the river and build "a permanent memorial" (Jos 4:7 NLT). That way when they were tempted to forget His goodness or doubt His faithfulness, they could look back and say, "Thus far has the Lord helped us" (1Sa 7:12 NIV).

Spurgeon said, "The words 'Thus far' are like a hand pointing in the direction of the past, through poverty and wealth, sickness and health, joy and sorrow – 'Thus far hath the Lord helped us!' Be strong and take heart for the Lord who 'thus far' has helped you, will help you all your journey through."

After her husband died on board the space shuttle, people would ask Evelyn Husband, "Where do you find such strength?" For her, it came from having experienced God's comfort. She says, "I knew God was going to walk me through this because He'd walked me through other things before. So often I've had to take hold of His hand and step out in faith into absolute blackness.

"I've gone way beyond the polite stages with God. I've yelled and cried out to Him with a deeper, gut-wrenching cry than ever before. But He's proven to me that He's there, holding my hand as I take each step forward. That's why when you walk through a crisis it's important to have your foundation of faith already established. *You have to know whose hand you're holding!*

"You stop fretting not because you know how things are going to work out, but because you know the God who'll work them out! That's why it's good to look back and identify what it was that helped you deal with past losses; things like faith in God, the love and support of friends and family, prayer, meditating on God's Word, reaching out to others who are hurting."

As creatures of habit we're inclined to keep using the coping skills, good and bad, given to us earlier in life. And when they're healthy it's good to reinforce them, but when they're working against us, we need to find new and better ones.

Many of us were told that because we were Christians, grieving demonstrated a lack of faith in God. One hospital chaplain tells of a lady who showed little sign of emotion as her husband was dying. One night as his death drew closer she began to cry quietly into her handkerchief to hide her tears. Just then her pastor arrived and in a loud voice announced, "Mrs. White's a good Christian. She knows God wipes away every tear and keeps us from feeling sorry for ourselves." Obviously he'd forgotten that "Jesus wept" at the grave of his friend Lazarus!

Your *faith* in God tells you about resurrection and new life, but your *humanity* tells you that you need to grieve in order to process your loss.

In ancient times bottles called lachrymatories were used to collect the tears of those in mourning. These were then placed inside the tomb of the deceased as a sign of respect. That custom may have inspired the Psalmist to write, "You keep track of all my sorrows. You have collected all my tears in your bottle...recorded each one in your book" (Ps 56:8 NLT). Sir Alexander Fleming, the English scientist, believed that tears were efficient microbe killers and demonstrated that just one teaspoon had enough antiseptic power to purify 100 gallons of water. Maybe we should all cry more often – for our health's sake!

So, how do you carry on when the flowers

have wilted and the grass has grown over the grave? What's the secret to pressing on when the bottom has dropped out? Let's look at the life of King David.

Returning from battle he and his troops found their homes in smoking ruins, their families taken captive by the enemy. The Bible says, "Then David and the men with him lifted up their voices and wept until they had no more strength to weep" (1Sa 30:4 AMP).

If ever there was ever a moment when David felt like throwing in the towel, it was now. But instead he "encouraged and strengthened himself in the Lord" (1Sa 30:6 AMP). How? By doing 4 important things: (1) Pouring out His heart to God. (2) Refusing to surrender to despair. (3) Focusing on the future. (4) Taking action. Listen: "David inquired at the Lord, saying, 'Shall I pursue after this troop? shall I overtake them?' And he answered him, 'Pursue: for thou shalt surely overtake them, and without fail recover all" (1Sa 30:8).

When you start feeling bogged down two things happen. First you begin to blame others and that leads to bitterness. Second you surrender to self-pity and that immobilizes you. Instead of railing against God or just giving up, David gained fresh perspective by looking beyond his pain and acknowledging that God's in control of every situation.

You see, life's not the way it's supposed to be, it's the way it is. How you handle it is what makes the difference! Our greatest victories come from our most painful experiences. Frederick Buechner says, "Even the saddest things, once we have made peace with them, can become sources of wisdom and strength for the journey that still lies ahead."

Jesus said that the rain falls "on the just and...unjust" (Mt 5:45). Loss comes to us all. Nobody's immune. Nobody gets off for good behavior. Solomon writes, "There is a...season for every activity...a time to be born and a time to die...a time to cry and a time to laugh. A time to grieve and a time to dance" (Ecc 3:1-4 NLT). Life is lived in seasons. And seasons have beginnings and endings. They cannot be rushed or shortened. Martin Luther said, "God writes the promise of resurrection not in books alone, but in every leaf of springtime." Loss is part of life. And, hard as it is to accept, new life only comes when you can release that which was there before.

But underlying the pain of loss, God remains constant. Listen to these Scriptures: "The mountains may depart and the hills disappear, but my kindness shall not leave you. My promise of peace for you will never be broken, says the Lord who has mercy upon you" (Is 54:10 TLB). "I will comfort you there as a child is comforted by its mother" (Is 66:13 NLT). "He will remove all...sorrows, and there will be no more death...or crying or pain" (Rev 21:4 NLT). "He is the source of every mercy and the

God who comforts us" (2Co 1:3 NLT). "Nothing in all creation will ever be able to separate us from the love of God" (Ro 8:39 NLT). "The Lord is my Strength...my heart...confidently leans on Him, and I am helped" (Ps 28:7 AMP).

In his book, "Is There Any Comfort?" John Hannah writes, "As I was preparing my sermon yesterday, the telephone rang and a student said, 'Last night my child died.' What could I say to him? I will say to him what I would say to anyone! It's captured in the words of this well-known hymn:

> When darkness seems to veil His face,
> I rest on His unchanging grace.
> When all around my soul gives way,
> He then is all my hope and stay.
>
> On Christ the solid rock I stand,
> all other ground is sinking sand,
> all other ground is sinking sand.

In 1871 when fire ravaged the city of Chicago leaving three hundred dead and one hundred thousand homeless, attorney Horatio Gates Spafford, a friend of D.L. Moody, helped its people get back on their feet. After two years of such work he and his family decided to take a much-needed vacation. They planned to travel to England to join Moody in an evangelistic crusade; then go on to Europe. When Spafford got delayed he sent his family ahead, planning to meet them on the other side of the Atlantic.

But they never made it. Near Newfoundland their ship collided with an English sailing vessel and sank within twenty minutes. Spafford's wife Anna survived by clinging to some floating wreckage, but all four of their daughters drowned. The next day Spafford received this terrible two-word telegram from his wife, *"Saved alone!"* and immediately went to be with her.

Later, in the course of relaying their tragic story to D.L. Moody, Spafford said quietly, "It is well. The will of God be done." In fact, it was those days of overwhelming grief that

inspired him to compose a beloved hymn
that has comforted so many of us:

> When peace like a river attendeth my way,
> When sorrows like sea-billows roll;
> Whatever my lot, Thou hast taught me to say:
> "It is well, it is well with my soul!"

"Ultimately, mourning means facing what wounds us, in the presence of the One who can heal us."

– Henry Nouwen

3
WHERE'S GOD IN ALL OF THIS?

"I can never get away from your presence!"
– Psalm 139:7-10 NLT

At one of his lowest points David cried, "God...Why do you remain so distant?... Every day I call...but you do not answer. Every night you hear my voice, but I find no relief" (Ps 22:1-2 NLT).

If you've suffered a painful loss, chances are, you can relate to those words. Sometimes it just feels like God's moved house and left no forwarding address! What does it mean when He's silent? What's He up to? Well, here are five insights we can gain from His silence:

1. His silence is not absence. David said, "I can never...get away from your presence!" (Ps 139:7 NLT). You have to feel secure with somebody in order to just sit quietly with them. Silence takes the emphasis off words; it builds an intimacy where they're no longer necessary. So if you want to be comfortable around God, learn to enter into silence with Him.

2. *His silence tests our trust level.* How much trust is actually involved if somebody's coaching your every step? It's like a parent running alongside a child who's learning to ride a bike. Right now the child lacks confidence, but he's going to look strange at fifty if his dad's still trotting along beside him! At some point God takes his hand off the wheel – and for a while it'll be a wobbly ride!

3. *His silence doesn't mean nothing's happening.* Have you ever tried to sit and watch a seed grow? You can't, can you? It stays in the earth till the time's right for it to emerge. And because you too have things planted deep inside, you must sit quietly before God in order for them to surface and grow. Some issues are buried so deep that only silence can force them to the surface so

that God – and you – can deal with them.

4. His silence isn't denial. The Bible says, "It is wrong to say God doesn't listen...the Almighty isn't concerned" (Job 35:13 NLT). Charles Trumbull says, "God knows when to withhold and when to grant visible signs of encouragement. It's good when He sends confirmation, but we grow faster when we've trusted Him without it. Those who do always receive the greatest evidence of His love." God answers every prayer; it's just that across some He writes, "The time has not yet come."

5. His silence won't last forever. "How long will it last?" you ask. It takes as long as it takes – and feels scary much of the time! But by letting God work you realize you're not alone; you develop a deeper intimacy with Him; and you discover that you can trust Him for the entire journey.

Henri Nouwen writes, "We wonder when grief hits hard and hurts deeply, why such a thing happened. To reveal God's glory? To remind us of the fragility of life? To deepen the faith of those who carry on? It's hard to answer 'Yes,' when everything seems dark...the important thing to us at that moment is to be relieved of the pain. But when we walk through the suffering rather than trying to avoid it, we greet it differently. We become willing to let it teach us. We see how God can use it for some larger end. *Ultimately, mourning means facing what wounds us, in the presence of the One who can heal us.*"

Because grief is painful and takes so much emotional energy, our initial reaction is to try and make it go away. That's why those in mourning talk about experiencing a sense of unreality and describe it as "a bad dream." However, once the numbness that protects us from being overwhelmed starts to recede, we come face-to-face with the gaping hole in our heart. That's when you can start to feel even worse. And when the loss was unexpected, it takes still more time to come to grips with it.

The key to finding your way out of the woods, is understanding where you are to begin with.

When you lose someone you love, you lose not only that person, but all the things associated with them. Things like: financial security, shared hopes and dreams, companionship, support, their personal interest in you, a sense of the future. Only when you come to recognize and accept how much your life will actually be affected by your loss, can you begin to move through it to a new beginning.

It's helpful to keep a journal where you can pour out your pain in private. Healing begins with accepting your loss and recognizing its significance in your life. Keep writing until you're ready to say, "With God's help I'll walk *through* this, not *around* it, and I'll look for the blessing it holds for me." Recognize the various ways in which your chief loss has caused lesser losses. Write them down so that you can pray specifically about them as they surface. Realize that it's okay to feel what you feel and that you don't have to tell people you're "fine" when you're having a bad day.

Grieving is hard work. Rabbi David Wolpe says, "When we experience loss, a hole opens up inside of us. It's almost as if the loss itself plows right through us, leaving us gasping for air. We bleed through that opening and sometimes old wounds are reopened. Things we thought were safely hidden inside, patched over and healed, prove painful again in the wake of the new loss."

Loss either leads to new life and growth – or it can destroy you. Jack Welch, former CEO of General Electric, grew up as a devoted Irish-Catholic. As a child he was an altar boy. Later as an adult he sometimes traveled an hour to attend church. But Welch's commitment to his faith changed thirty-four years ago when his mother died suddenly of a heart attack. He says, "I felt cheated, angry and mad at God for taking my mother away." And while he still claims to believe in God, he no longer attends church and says he's "lost his heart for religion."

A few years ago, baseball pitching-ace, Donny Moore, couldn't live with the aftermath of losing an all-important game in the American League play-offs. So he shot his wife and then himself. Compare that to star baseball player, Dave Dravecky, who not only lost his career, but his pitching arm and his shoulder to cancer. What did he do? He founded *Outreach of Hope Ministries,* and now travels the world telling others about a God who offers us beauty in exchange for ashes.

Writer Kenneth Wilson tells how he slept in the attic of his family's four-story home. As the youngest, he went to bed first – and it felt like a long way to the top of those stairs! Especially since there was no electricity up there and a gas light had to be turned on, then turned off again once he was settled.

He writes: "That room seemed to be at the end of the earth, close to unexplained noises and dark secrets. My father would try to stop the windows from rattling by wedging matchsticks into the cracks. But they rattled in spite of his efforts. Sometimes he'd read me a story. But inevitably the time would come when he would turn out the light, shut the door, and I'd hear his steps on the stairs, growing fainter and fainter. Then all would be quiet except for the rattling windows – and my cowering imagination.

"Once I remember my father asking, 'Would you rather I leave the light on and go downstairs, or turn the light out and stay with you for a while?' I chose his presence in the darkness over his absence with the light."

And isn't that what we want most; the assurance that God is there?

During a recent upheaval in the Middle

East, Ron Jones, who serves with the Christian Missionary Alliance Church in Israel, shared the following in a prayer letter, "Several times we have come into closer contact with this conflict than our comfort zone allowed. Yesterday a friend shared with us something that was a delightful reminder of God's care for us. She watched a shepherd tending his flock near the area where the guns are fired. Every time the shots rang out the sheep scattered in fright. The shepherd then touched each of them with his staff, spoke calmly, and the sheep settled down because they trusted him. Then another shot sounded and the same routine happened all over again. Each time the sheep needed the shepherd to reassure them they were safe."

David said, "Yea, though I walk through the valley of the shadow of death, I will fear no evil; For You are with me; Your rod and Your staff, they comfort me" (Ps 23:4 NKJV). God's love is never measured by our comfort. Just like the sheep in the story, our

Shepherd is always with us. We never have to wonder where He is or worry that He'll abandon us when the going gets rough.

Furthermore, He knows that the only way to get you to where He wants you to be, is through the valley – not around it. That's why He goes *before* you, walks *beside* you, and comes *behind* you. In the valley you'll experience His love in a way you've never known it before. And you need to "fear no evil," because nothing intimidates the One who died for you, rose again for you, and promises "Because I live, you shall live also" (Jn 14:19 NKJV).

So remember, your tomorrows aren't in the hands of your boss, your banker, your broker, or anybody else. They're in *God's* hands; and He'll be there for you when every other support has gone. *Think: hasn't He always taken care of you?*

"No person's grief...occurs in a vacuum.
It's influenced, shaped and determined
by a constellation of factions that
combine to make their response...
as individual as a fingerprint."

–Therese Rando

4
KEEP WALKING!

"I will turn their mourning into joy..."
                    –Jeremiah 31:13 NLT

The Greek philosopher, Heracleitus, said, "There is nothing permanent in life except change." And even though we know that's true, still we cling to the notion that somehow we'll make it through life without losing what we love along the way.

Author and motivational speaker Zig Ziglar says, "The longest twenty-four hours of my life were those right after my daughter's death. When making her funeral arrangements I had to listen to a salesman who was an incessant talker and told us thirty times that he wasn't a salesman. Twice I had to leave the room; I simply couldn't handle him.

"The night before, half asleep and half awake, I kept thinking my daughter was wondering when her daddy was going to come and get her. The next morning I took a walk, praying and crying the whole way. When I returned the Lord spoke to me in such a distinct way: 'She's fine. She's with me. And you're going to be fine too. I'm all you need. Keep walking. Keep talking. Keep praying. Keep crying.'"

Rabbi David Wolpe says, "The frightening thing about loss is what we do to ourselves to avoid it. We know we can't live without losing, but this knowledge doesn't prevent us from seeking to protect ourselves. So we narrow our souls. We draw ourselves tighter and tighter. No longer open to the world with all its hurts, we feel safe."

Then when grief *does* hit, our world falls apart. We can't believe it happened. We feel out of control, physically and emotionally exhausted. We sigh a lot and feel like sleeping all the time. We experience a constant lump in our throat and a hole in our stomach. We overeat or else we don't eat enough. As constant waves of anxiety threaten to drown us, we just want to give up and die because it feels like life's over and we'll never be happy again.

No two people grieve in exactly the same way!

Just as every relationship is unique, so is the mourning that follows its loss. Therese Rando says, "No person's grief...occurs in a vacuum. It's influenced, shaped and determined by a constellation of factions that combine to make their response...as individual as a fingerprint."

There are many things in life you can predict, but not your response to loss. In one bereavement group a woman named Chris said, "I need to believe God took my husband. That's the only way I can accept his death. If I thought God didn't have anything to do with it I couldn't bear it." Another woman responded, "Oh, not me! I don't for a minute think God comes and takes people away. I think that's just the way it is in life. We live and we die, and God walks right along with us, helping us when times are hard and we have to let go of somebody. A third woman, Cathy, added, "You may both be right. All I know is that God loves us and I turn to Him for help in all my troubles." All three responses are examples of how, as individuals we see God's hand in our circumstances as we try to make sense of suffering. And all three are as valid as they are varied.

Jesus said, "Blessed are those who mourn, For they shall be comforted" (Mt 5:4 NKJV), because grief and loss are experiences that can't be "solved." Most of us have become skilled at finding quick solutions to our problems. In fact, we think there's something wrong with us when we can't "fix" ourselves quickly enough. The Swiss psychiatrist, Carl Jung, said, "We instinctively refuse to try the way that leads through the darkness. We wish only to hear of unequivocal results, and completely forget that these results can only be brought about when we have ventured into and emerged from the darkness."

Emotions are the "vital signs" of life; we all have them. But because many of us grew up hearing phrases like, "Don't cry"... "Don't be angry"..."Stop feeling sorry for yourself," we deny what we're really feeling and try to appear "strong" for others. But what we resist persists! Struggling to squelch our emotions has the opposite effect. Unexpressed feelings don't disappear, they just go underground and come back as guilt, depression, rage, addiction, shame, and denial. Only when you stop fighting and allow them to surface and be processed in healthy ways, do they diminish.

Grieving lets you accept your emotions as they arise; to express your pain and move beyond it.

Recovery doesn't happen overnight; it

happens in proportion to the significance of your loss. Only small losses are grieved and healed quickly.

Gerald Sittser says, "Willingness to face the loss and to enter into the darkness is the first step we must take. And like all first steps, it's probably the most difficult and takes the most time."

Pastor Mark Coleman's son, Peter, inherited his dad's love for hiking. When he was just five-years-old the pair planned to hike around a mountain and camp beside the lake. Mark told his son it would be a tough hike, and although they'd be tired they'd have to keep walking to make camp before dark.

But it was even longer and harder than they expected. The little boy grew weary – but he kept walking. He slipped on loose rocks – but he kept going. He fell and ripped the knee out of his jeans – but he plodded on. Finally, after one slip too many, he sat down on a big rock and started to cry. When his dad approached and started to say something, Peter cut him off, saying, "I know, Dad, it's okay to cry – as long as I just keep walking!"

Paul says, "We get knocked down, but we get up...and keep going...We don't look at the troubles we can see right now...we look forward to what we have not yet seen. For the troubles we see will soon be over, but the joys to come...last forever" (2Co 4:9,18 NLT). When the journey's long and hard it's okay to stop and rest – even cry – so long as you keep walking. "How can I do it?" you ask. By "keeping [your] eyes on Jesus...from start to finish" (Heb 12:2 NLT), and allowing Him to be your example, your comforter, and your motivator.

When you feel all alone remember, God's as close as a prayer. He says, "Do not be afraid...I will be with you. When you go through rivers of difficulty, you will not drown! When you walk through the fire...the flames will not consume you.

for...you are precious to me...I love you" (Is 43:1-4 NLT).

Grieving is the process by which you adjust to loss and start putting your life back together. And even though it wasn't an experience you'd ever choose, eventually you'll start to feel better. The Bible says, "Weeping may endure for a night, but joy comes in the morning" (Ps 30:5 AMP).

Your joy will return – God promises it!

"Willingness to face the loss and to enter into the darkness is the first step we must take. And like all first steps, it's probably the most difficult and takes the most time."

—Gerald Sittser

5
DON'T RUSH TO CLOSURE

*"When they walk through the Valley
of Weeping [they]...grow stronger"*
—Psalm 84:6-7 NLT

God doesn't lift us out of our grief, He takes us through it and makes us stronger! Walking through the "Valley of Weeping" means feeling, dealing and healing. When you rush to premature closure you end up burying things that'll rise again. Until you can honestly acknowledge what happened to you, your future responses won't be based in reality or lead to emotional wholeness.

I know. As a thirteen year-old boy standing beside my father's grave in Belfast, Northern Ireland, loving, well-intentioned relatives who knew no better, patted me on the head and said, "Be a good soldier — don't cry!"

And I didn't.

Thirty years later, after wrestling with compulsions that almost destroyed me, I ended up one night on the floor of my home, fetal and sobbing, as I expressed my long overdue grief. It was the first step in a process that lasted until I was able to revisit my father's grave and say what I needed to say. Once that happened a chain broke, I was released, the child within me started to grow up, and my un-dealt with wounds began to heal.

It was the beginning of the rest of my life!

As long as I kept buried within me the sense of loss I experienced and the anger I felt toward God for permitting it, it kept resurrecting itself in harmful ways.

But when I embraced it, I dethroned it.

Jesus said, "You shall know the truth, and the truth shall make you free" (Jn 8:32 NKJV). It's not time that heals; it's insight! It's knowing and embracing the truth, including its painful aspects – that sets you free.

Plus, until you embrace your own pain, you'll never be able to empathize with anyone else's. You'll offer hollow words and hand out shallow prescriptions that didn't work for you and won't work for them either. How else could Jesus be "touched with the feeling of our infirmities" (Heb 4:15), without first embracing His own?

Awareness is the beginning of inner healing.

Only as we become aware of the issues in our lives, do we find a roadmap to wholeness. As God's children we're not exempt from the universally-recognized stages of grief:

1. **Denial:** "It's not real. It can't be happening."

2. **Anger:** "It's not fair. Why's God letting this happen to me?"

3. **Bargaining:** "I'll do anything, just make it go away."

4. **Depression:** Silence and withdrawal.

5. **Acceptance:** "I want your will, not mine" (Mt 26:39 NLT).

Whether it's the loss of your child, your marriage, your career, your health, or anything else you value, when you turn to God He'll give you the grace to embrace it, grieve it, express it, release it, and "go from strength to strength" (Ps 84:7).

Sometimes we try to release things before we've experienced them, because we fear *the process*!

Or like me, you've been taught that expressing your feelings is a sign of weakness. No, the opposite is true! By stuffing your pain into an emotional garbage can, you end up squandering precious time and energy sitting on the lid, trying to keep the contents from spilling out.

In *A Better Kind of Grieving*, Bill Hybels

writes: "Fifty years ago, industrialists thought they could just bury toxic waste and it would go away. But we have since learned it doesn't. It leaks into the water, contaminates crops and kills animals. And burying grief does the same thing. It leaks into our emotional system and wreaks havoc. It distorts our perceptions of life and taints our relationships.

"I had lunch with a seasoned counselor this week and asked her what she advised people to do when they're dealing with loss. She said, 'Of course I tell them to feel their feelings. But I also urge them to: (1) radically reduce the pace of their lives; (2) review their loss and talk about it openly; (3) think and write about it reflectively. (4) pray it through.

'It's been my experience that most people want to *run* from their pain...to *replace* it with another feeling as soon as they can. You can use alcohol, sex, money, or stay so busy that you don't have to feel anything. Or with God's help, you can feel the pain, let it go and move forward.'"

Hybels continues, "I didn't do that when my father died. I replaced the pain real fast. I think I missed only four days of work. I just replaced the feeling of loss and disappointment with a frenzied ministry schedule. I ran from it. That was a bad move for me, and for other people around me."

Some people get through things quickly. Some never do! They speak only of the past because they've never gotten beyond it. Or they're afraid if they stop grieving it'll appear as though they've forgotten their loved one or didn't really love them.

Are you running from your pain today? Are you trading it in prematurely for some other feeling? That's not God's way! Listen, "You will weep and mourn...but [eventually] your grief will turn to joy...and no one will take [it] away" (Jn 16:20-22 NIV).

Moses wasn't just the greatest leader the

children of Israel had ever known, he was the *only* one. His death was an unspeakable loss. How could God let this happen? Especially since they hadn't yet entered The Promised Land. A nation's dream was shattered, its heart broken, its confidence shaken. At that moment of unprecedented emotional upheaval, Israeli life – social, political, and commercial – ground to a halt while they poured out their collective pain and wept together on the Plains of Moab. For thirty days and nights God stood by and allowed them to mourn in a healthy expression of legitimate grief. No hurrying...no divine censuring...no denial. Just feeling – making way for healing.

Only when God saw that they'd completed the process, did He tell Joshua to lead them forward.

They had to go through, to get through!

Then we read, "After the death of Moses...the Lord spoke to Joshua...saying: 'Moses My servant is dead. Now, therefore, arise, go over this Jordan, you and all this people, to the land which I am giving to them...Every place that the sole of your foot will tread upon I have given you...as I was with Moses, so will I be with you. I will not leave you nor forsake you...Have I not commanded you? Be strong and of good courage; do not be afraid, nor be dismayed, for the Lord your God is with you wherever you go" (Jos 1:1-9 NKJV).

And do you know what? The God who spoke those words to Joshua – is *your* God too!

*"The turning point in grief is marked
with a decision either to move forward...
or to remain in the status quo
not making changes."*

— *Catherine Saunders*

6
INCHING BACK INTO LIFE

*"You will have courage because
you will have hope."*
– Job 11:18 NLT

Tom was deeply depressed following his wife's death. For an hour he poured out his heart. Now, while catharsis is good and can show what still needs to be healed, talk alone won't change anything. So I asked him, "If the situation was reversed and you'd gone to heaven first, what would you want Ellie to do?" Immediately he replied, "Go on and enjoy life." The second he verbalized it the lights came on and he exclaimed, "I've been feeling sorry for myself too long. We both hated it when people did that. I'm going to reconnect, find fresh purpose and get back to church!" He did, and the next time we talked he'd started to rebuild his life. The pain was still there, but he'd begun to transcend it by taking action.

When your life's been up-ended by loss, you just want to withdraw from everything. And at first that may be what you need to do, because you've no energy or desire to do anything else. Then after the initial sense of disbelief begins to dissipate, you begin to ride an emotional roller coaster where you struggle to process all the implications of your loss. Eventually, however, as you give yourself time and space, you come to a point where you're ready to start inching back into life.

Catherine Saunders says, "The turning point in grief is marked with a decision to either move forward...or to remain in the status quo, not making changes." When that happens you can opt to do one of three things: (1) Stay as you are and insist that nothing's changed. (2) Continue to withdraw and begin a downward spiral away from life. (3) Draw on God's grace and begin living again.

One woman told her support group, "One day the thought came into my mind that I might start getting through this; that it was time. At first I pushed it away. It felt like I was being disloyal to my husband. I was afraid I'd forget him if I stopped grieving. But gradually it just felt like I needed to move in that direction – that it was the right thing to do."

James Hollis says, "No one is free until they can say...'I am not what happened to me; I am what I choose to become.'" Too often we live our lives the way we read a novel – waiting to see how it all turns out. No, *you're* the one writing the next chapter, and you've got a lot to say about where you go from here! You can't change the reality of your loss, but you can allow your past to rob you of your future. Don't let that happen!

In the Old Testament Moses issued this challenge to the children of Israel, "I have given you the choice between life and death...choose life" (Dt 30:19 NLT). And each day you face that same choice. There's no getting off the hook.

Don't stay so long in the past that the future's gone before you get there. God has promised to " turn [your] mourning into joy...and exchange...sorrow for rejoicing" (Jer 31:13 NLT). He can help you bounce back, by taking your painful memories and turning them into powerful motivators and sources of future wisdom.

Paul says God "comforts us in all our troubles so...we will be able to give [others] the same comfort" (2Co 1:4 NLT). One of the surest roads to recovery is through helping others. In fact, we were born with a natural empathy for those who are hurting; even babies in a nursery start crying when other infants cry. Compassion, which literally means "to suffer with," is the ability to be moved by the troubles of others. When we reach from out of our own pain to help others, it comes back to us in healing and a sense of wholeness. Jack Kornfield says, "You take it all in. You let the pain of life touch your heart and you turn it into compassion. What a splendid way to move through the world, bringing blessings to all we touch."

Karl Menninger, the famous psychiatrist, was once asked what he would tell someone on the verge of a nervous breakdown. Surprisingly, instead of advising him to seek psychiatric help, Menninger said he'd tell him, "Lock up your house, go across the railway tracks, find someone in need and do something to help them." One of the wonderful results of compassion is – the healing of your own grief! It's a two-way street where the giver receives and the receiver gives. What's so great about hugging somebody else is, you get hugged too!

Are you afraid you won't know what to say? Don't be! Scott Peck says, "The most loving thing we can do when a friend is in pain, is to share the pain – to be there even when we have nothing to offer except our presence, and even when being there is painful to ourselves." One cancer patient said, "What helps me the most is just having somebody try to understand what I'm feeling." Another said, "Just sit here and let me hold your hand. It helps when someone's close."

A woman whose husband died wrote a letter to an advice columnist called, *"The Story of Widowhood."* The letter reads: "First numbness, then busyness. A million things to settle. Endless death certificates and things to sign. Friends are so considerate; caring support from relatives. You keep busy.

"But at night you pound the empty side of the bed in grief. Finally you close your eyes, throw his toothbrush into the garbage and toss out the old work shoes you brought home from the hospital in a plastic bag. You empty the closet and give all his things away. It's a heartache like you wouldn't believe.

Every suit reminds you of a special place or time you shared together.

"A year has passed; you're still in one piece. Then the blow! Your friends celebrate a birthday – *all couples*. You're not included because you'd be a 'fifth wheel.' Some wives even consider you a threat. Please remember us. Don't treat us like excess baggage. We've been handed a rotten break and we need friends. Signed – *Forgotten*."

After Ray and Judy Williamson's son, David, was killed in a fall, Ray said, "I used to wonder if I should go to the funeral home when somebody had a tragedy, because I always feel so awkward and don't know what to say. But I'll never ask again. I'll always go. It's not what you say, but your presence that makes the difference."

When two teenagers died in a car accident, their parents decided to have a joint wake. Over one thousand people attended, some waiting up to three hours to comfort the bereaved families. When one man, who'd stood by himself in the line finally reached the front, he said, "I didn't know your children and I've never met you. But I came here tonight because I'd a son who died two years ago. I know how it feels. In the days ahead you'll go through every emotion you can imagine. I just want you to know that I'm here for you if you ever need to talk." Then he pressed his card into their hand and walked away.

A stranger gave three hours of his time to people he didn't know because he wanted to help them through the most tragic experience of their lives.

Why? Because it's in reaching out to others that we ourselves become whole!

"I have hope because the Bible speaks about our bodies being glorified. I know the meaning of that now. It's the time after my death, when I – the quadriplegic – will be on my feet dancing."

– Joni Eareckson Tada

7

WILL WE SEE OUR LOVED ONES AGAIN?

*"The tent we live in here...will be destroyed.
But...God will have...for us...a home in
heaven that will last forever."*

– 11 Corinthians 5:1 NCV

On September 11, 2001, people from all walks of life found themselves with multiple funerals to attend; their photograph albums filled with the smiling faces of dead people.

When the grieving mother of three preschoolers told them their dad, a New York City policeman, wouldn't be coming home because he'd gone to heaven, her tearful four year-old asked, "Can we call him on his cell phone?" "No," she replied, searching desperately for words, "but someday we'll go to heaven and see him." "Will it be a long time? Will he remember us? Will he still be a policeman?" Then after a pause that seemed to last forever, the little girl asked, "Mommy, where's heaven? What's it like?"

Who's qualified to answer that question? Only someone who's been there – and two people fit the bill:

1. The Apostle Paul: After visiting heaven he described it as, "one huge family reunion." He writes, "We can tell you with complete confidence...that when the Master comes again to get us, those of us who are still alive, will not get a jump on the dead and leave them behind. In actual fact, they'll be ahead of us. The Master himself will...come down from heaven and the dead in Christ will rise – they'll go first...the rest of us...will be caught up with them...to meet the Master...then there will be one huge family reunion" (1Th 4:15-18 TM).

"But how can we be sure?" you ask. Because at the cross a showdown took place when Jesus called Satan's hand. Tired of seeing us intimidated, He walked into a tomb, turned it into a lighted underpass to heaven, emerged victorious and announced, "Death, who's afraid of you now?" (1Co 15:55 TM).

2. Jesus Christ: He said, "Let not your heart be troubled; you believe in God, believe also in Me. In My Father's house are many mansions; if it were not so, I would have told you. I go to prepare a place for you. And if I go and prepare a place for you, I will come again and receive you to Myself; that where I am, there you may be also" (Jn 14:1-3 NKJV).

A woman who loved flowers, planted a rare vine against a stonewall at the back of her garden. She nurtured it and it grew. But she was disappointed that it never bloomed. Then one day, as she was wondering what went wrong, the lady next door invited her over. When she got there her neighbor said, "I can't thank you enough for planting such a lovely vine. Look at the exquisite flowers, they smell wonderful!" Unbeknown to the woman who'd planted it, the vine had crept over the wall and was in full bloom on the other side – she just couldn't see it from her perspective.

John says that even though we're "already God's children...we can't even imagine what we will be like when Christ returns. But we do know that when he comes we will be like him, for we will see him as he really is" (1Jn 3:2 NLT).

"What's heaven like?" you ask.

Think of...

> Holding a hand, and finding it's God's hand,
>
> Breathing new air, and finding it celestial air,
>
> Feeling invigorated, and finding it immortality,
>
> Passing from storm to tempest to unknown calm,
>
> Waking up, and finding it home.

"God shall wipe away all tears from their eyes; and there shall be no more death, neither sorrow, nor crying, neither shall there be any more pain; for the former things are passed away."

– *Revelation 21:4*

8
RUTH'S STORY

"In my father's house are many mansions...
I go to prepare a place for you."
— John 14:2

When my mother passed away, my sister Ruth had a remarkable experience. I've asked her to share it with you:

"My mother died in 1990, a few days shy of turning seventy-four. When we buried her on her birthday, I remember thinking it strange that she came into the world and left on exactly the same date. But then, very little was 'usual' about my mother, so it shouldn't have surprised me!

"The Sunday before she was hospitalized with a heart attack, she attended two church services and was in great spirits. Even on Monday when she was admitted to the

Coronary Care Unit she insisted she couldn't have had a heart attack, and felt as though she could, 'get up and dance around the room.' Four days later she was doing so well that the doctors planned on moving her to a regular room. They told me that's where she'd be when I came to visit that evening.

"Earlier in the day she'd asked me to stop by a bakery and get her some of her favorite cookies for a bedtime 'cuppa tea.' So as a result, I was twenty minutes late getting to the hospital.

"When I got there and the nurse said the doctor needed to talk to me, I wasn't overly concerned. I thought he just wanted to give me an update. Even when he came into the room looking very serious, it still didn't register. In fact, when he said, 'I'm very sorry, there was nothing more we could do, it happened very fast,' I thought he was referring to some other patient. So I said, 'Oh, you must have me confused with someone else. My mother just got out of

CCU today because she was doing so well. It can't be her.' But it was.

"Apparently she'd had another heart attack. The doctor described it as a 'massive blowout,' just like you'd get on a faulty tire.

"When I went into her room she was still hooked up to the machines. But I knew she was gone because the light in her eyes had gone out. I remember being surprised that the nurse was crying. I asked, 'How can you do this job if you get so emotionally involved with your patients?' She replied, 'It's just that some of them touch your heart, and your mother was one of those people. We all loved her Irish accent.'

"One of my Mom's biggest concerns as she grew older was that she'd get sick and 'become a burden.' So it gave me some comfort to think that God had answered her prayer and taken her home, without prolonged suffering.

"But because everything happened so

fast, I was left with questions that haunted me. *Where was my mother now? Would I really see her again? Did she know how I felt?* I know as a Christian you're not supposed to have doubts, but I couldn't help wondering. I kept thinking, if only I hadn't stopped to pick up those cookies I'd have gotten to the hospital to see her before she died, and had a chance to say 'I love you, Ma.' But rarely, does life go the way we want or expect.

"Then one morning, weeks later, as I was sitting on the edge of the bed at home, my mother came into the room and sat down beside me. I don't know how else to describe it! Her expression was tranquil and her face had an 'upward,' heavenly appearance. If you think this sounds 'airy fairy,' trust me, I would have thought exactly the same before it happened to me! At that moment, however, I knew that this was God's way of letting me know she was in a place which Paul describes as 'far better' (See Col 1:21).

She stayed with me for a few seconds, holding me in her arms the way you'd cradle a baby. Then she looked into my face and said, 'You're worried because you didn't get to tell me you loved me the day I died. But don't be; I *know* you love me.' Then she was gone.

"To say I was startled would be an understatement; I'm just not the kind of person those things happen to! So I convinced myself that I'd imagined it. I was concerned that if I told anybody they'd question my sanity! So even though I felt *personally* comforted, I persuaded myself that the whole thing had stemmed from wishful thinking and an overactive imagination.

"But there was more to come!

"A couple of weeks later as I was planting flowers at her gravesite, I looked around and saw my mother's legs and feet standing beside me. Again, this was a very distinctive experience, because she was wearing what

I'd always jokingly referred to as her 'little old lady sneakers' – the ones she always wore when we went shopping. This time she said, 'Why seek ye the living among the dead? Don't you know I'm not in that 'wee box' in the ground, Ruth! My spirit's gone back to the God that gave it!' And with that she disappeared.

"I saw her one more time after that.

"Again it happened at the cemetery as I was filling a container used to water flowers. I looked up and there she was again. This time she was sitting in the passenger seat of my car. It wasn't spooky or weird as you might imagine – which is just as well, because as anybody who knows me well will tell you, I'm not the world's bravest soul!

"God knows what it takes to bring comfort and closure to each of us. And I just happen to be the kind of 'doubting Thomas' who likes to have proof. It's not a trait I'm particularly proud of, but I need to be honest because I suspect that some of you reading this probably feel the same way.

"At Mom's funeral service the pastor talked about how in Ireland she'd raised her three children in church. Apparently she told him that on the nights she worried because we were out late, she walked to the gate at the end of the path and looked down the road, waiting for us to come home. He speculated that in heaven, she was probably still walking to the gate, looking down the road to see if we were coming home. It's a picture that resonates with me to this day, and one I find comforting.

"Though I've never had any more visions of her, I no longer look at death in the same way. Just knowing that our loved ones are waiting to welcome us home, helps illuminate 'the valley of the shadow,' and remove the 'sting of death.'"

ACKNOWLEDGEMENTS

God Knows You're Grieving,
Joan Gunzelman. Sorin Books/Ave Maria Press, Notre Dame, In. 2001.

A Voice in the Wilderness,
Joseph Bayly. Cook Communications/ Scripture Press Publishers, Inc.
Colorado Springs, Colo. 2000.

Having Faith without Fear,
Kenneth L. Wilson. Harpers & Row, New York, NY. 1970

Holding onto Hope: Drawn by Suffering to the Heart of God,
Nancy Guthrie. Tyndale House, Cambridge, U.K. 2002.

Disciplines of the Christian Life,
Eric Liddell. Abingdon Press, Nashville, Tenn. 1985

Day by Day We Magnify Thee,
Martin Luther. Augsburg Fortress Publishers, Appleton, Wis. 1994

Beyond Ground Zero,
Bob Gass, Bridge-Logos Publishing, Gainesville, Florida. 2001.

A Better Kind Of Grieving,
Bill Hybels

Other Magazine Sources:
Leadership, Preaching Today, Christianity Today, Today's Christian Woman.

Notes

Notes